IDEAS FOR BUSINESS

----- ❧☙ -----

A scientific method to discover market demands and give people what they are willing to pay for

Do You Want To Stand Above Your Competitors And Getting Stuck in Your Costumers' Mind!?

https://goo.gl/dC3PC0

Do You Want To Know A Profitable Way To Make Money From Home For Real!?

https://goo.gl/cEVDkO

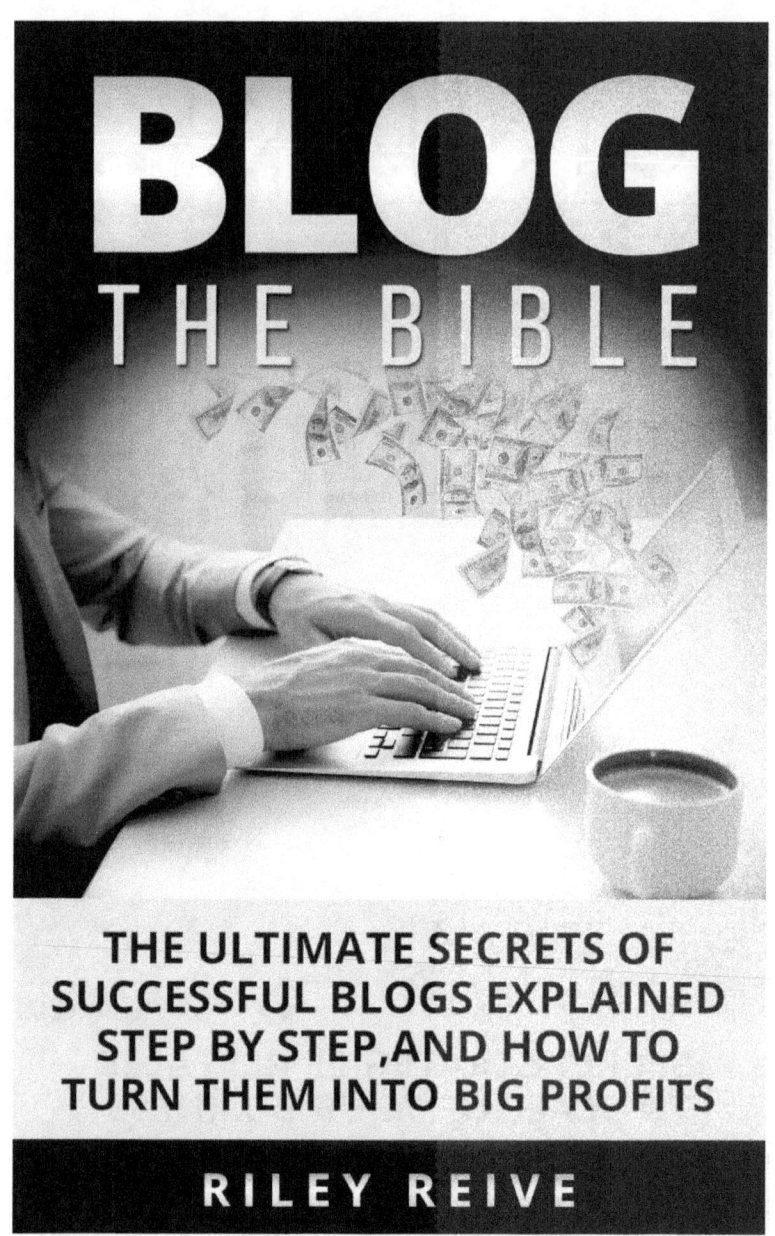

Would You Like To Blog On Almost Any Niche And Get Profit From It!?

https://goo.gl/o33rR5

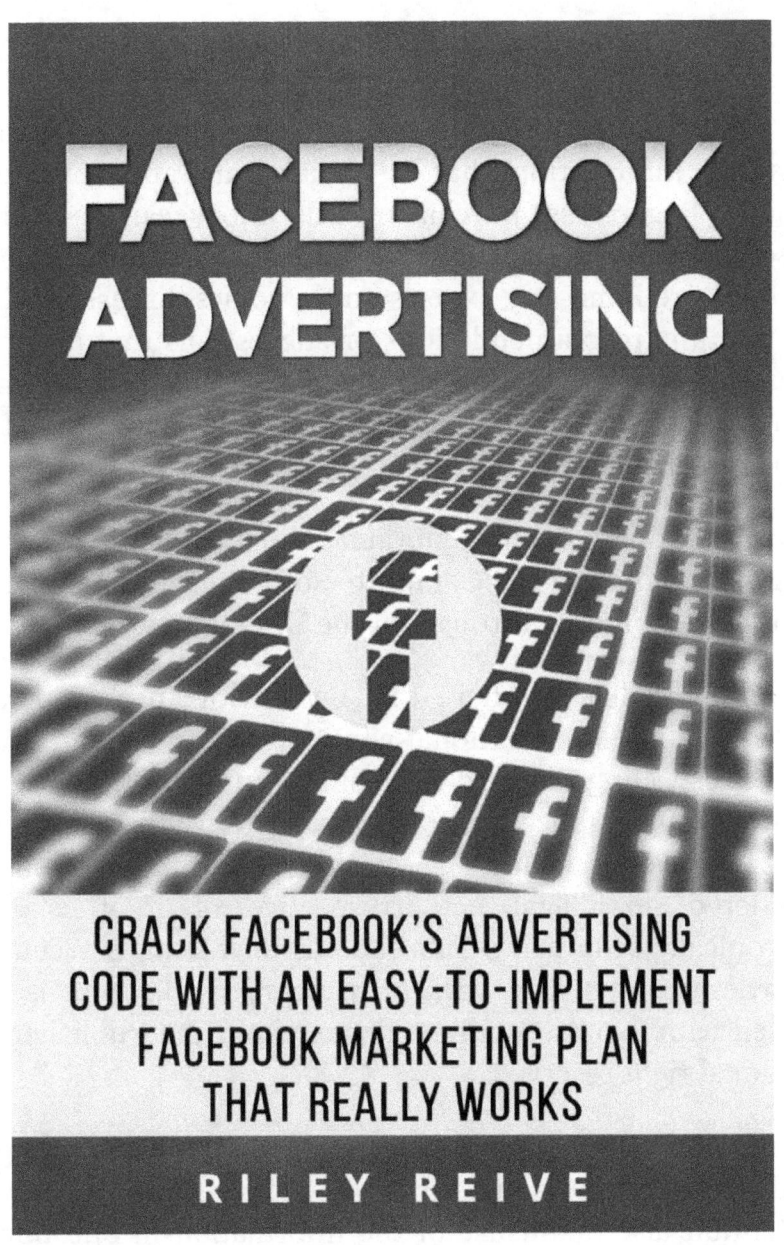

Are you looking for a powerful advertising system that brings you perfect and interested prospects for your business?

https://goo.gl/Yw9u0D

© **Copyright 2017 by Riley Reive - All rights reserved.**

The follow eBook is reproduced below with the goal of providing information that is as accurate and reliable as possible. Regardless, purchasing this eBook can be seen as consent to the fact that both the publisher and the author of this book are in no way experts on the topics discussed within and that any recommendations or suggestions that are made herein are for entertainment purposes only. Professionals should be consulted as needed prior to undertaking any of the action endorsed herein.

This declaration is deemed fair and valid by both the American Bar Association and the Committee of Publishers Association and is legally binding throughout the United States.

If you would like to share this book with another person, please purchase an additional copy for each recipient. Thank you for respecting the hard work of this author. Otherwise, the transmission, duplication or reproduction of any of the following work including specific information will be considered an illegal act irrespective of if it is done electronically or in print. This extends to creating a secondary or tertiary copy of the work or a recorded copy and is only allowed with express written consent from the Publisher. All additional right reserved.

The information in the following pages is broadly considered to be a truthful and accurate account of facts and as such any inattention, use or misuse of the information in question by the reader will render any resulting actions solely under their purview. There are no scenarios in which the publisher or the original author of this work can be in any fashion deemed liable for any hardship or damages that may befall them after undertaking information described herein.

Additionally, the information in the following pages is intended only for informational purposes and should thus be thought of as universal. As befitting its nature, it is presented without assurance regarding its prolonged validity or interim quality. Trademarks that are mentioned are done without written consent and can in no way be considered an endorsement from the trademark holder.

TABLE OF CONTENT

INTRODUCTION 1

CHAPTER 1: CREATING A NEW BUSINESS IDEA 3

CHAPTER 2: FINDING A KILLER BUSINESS IDEA 7

CHAPTER 3: HOW TO CREATE A PROFITABLE ONLINE BUSINESS IDEA? 13

CHAPTER 4: ASSESSING BUSINESS IDEAS THAT YOU HAVE GENERATED 23

CHAPTER 5: STEPS TO GENERATING YOUR NEXT SUCCESSFUL BUSINESS IDEA 31

CONCLUSION 41

INTRODUCTION

Ideation is the creative process of generating, developing, and communicating new business ideas.

When we plan to launch a new business, we either leverage an existing concept or we develop our own unique idea. The same applies to growing an existing business. I have always struggled with determining which is harder - finding the idea or executing on it.

Sometimes ideas are easy enough to conjure, and the hard part is deciding if it's good enough as the basis for developing a profitable business. If you have what you believe is a "great idea", the next challenge is to prove or test that it will translate into a successful venture.

Then there are times when a viable idea is the hardest thing to find. It may seem like all the good ideas are taken, and you are left on the sidelines with the resources and desire to start or grow a business but without a great idea.

The ideation process can take a day or it can take years, and as with the creative process, it's usually unproductive to rush it.

Aside from the other typical barriers of resources (money and people), the lack of a "good idea" is often what keeps people from taking action on their dream of becoming their own boss.

CHAPTER 1:

CREATING A NEW BUSINESS IDEA

Creating a new business starts with the idea. The process of developing that idea, and your business concept, may perhaps include some level of testing through prototyping and iteration.

During these early phases, your idea will undoubtedly evolve and may even morph into something entirely different. There are three basic categories for business ideas, and considering these categories can help with sparking that next great brainchild or validating your existing one:

1. New: A new invention or business idea. This is the most difficult category for new business ideas. There are very few truly and completely new ideas. By "new" I neither mean something that absolutely does not currently nor in the past exist in any way.

    It's easy to confuse a new idea with what is really an improvement or disruption of an existing or traditional way of doing something. Truly new and unique ideas are hard to come by, so don't get paralyzed by thinking this is the only source of viable new ideas.

CHAPTER 1: CREATING A NEW BUSINESS IDEA

2. Improvement: This is the proverbial better mouse trap. Examples include exterior express car washes (where you stay in the car), and LED lighting. Most small businesses probably fall into this category. You take an existing service or product and you make or deliver it in a better way, either directly or indirectly.

   You may make it of good quality raw materials, for example, or you may add value to the product or service by including additional services or add-ons.

3. Disruption: A new and revolutionary way of doing something. Examples include Uber, AirBnB, and Amazon. Our modern interconnected world - supported and made possible by the internet - now allows us to completely reinvent, transform and disrupt entire industries.

The internet and other technologies are not the only way to execute on a disruptive business idea, but it has certainly accelerated our ability to do so.

Where do great ideas come from? Sources of ideas can include reading, podcasts, art, architecture, personal experiences, travel, conversations, and hobbies, borrowing from others, crowd creativity, crowdsourcing, and attempting to solve existing problems in our world.

For existing businesses, the best source of ideas is usually your customers. Yet it takes a bit more than just experiencing or reading something to spark your next great idea.

Consciously and objectively experiencing new things will definitely influence and feed your creative abilities, and it's one of the most productive ways we can continue to develop our ability to generate great ideas.

IDEAS FOR BUSINESS

Does this mean that you have to be creative to generate good business ideas? I believe creativity is certainly one of the main ingredients required for ideation, along with ingenuity and vision.

The challenge for many people, however, is that they either have little confidence in their inherent creative abilities or don't have the courage to express and tap into it.

The idea generation process is much like the creative process in that we are putting forth something personal to be judged by others. You must have the courage and confidence to submit ideas that others might think are frivolous or ridiculous.

The ideal process is to identify one or more business ideas, test them, and then continue with developing the idea that has the best possibility for success. Of course, always remember that the true test of an idea's business viability ultimately rests entirely with the customer. Also remember that if your concept was easy, it would probably have already been done by someone else.

Some questions to ask yourself to help qualify your business idea:

1. What need does my product or service fill? What problem does it solve?

2. What are the features and benefits of my offering?

3. What is my competitive advantage? What makes this idea truly unique in my market?

4. How do my skills and experience fit with my idea?

CHAPTER 1: CREATING A NEW BUSINESS IDEA

5. How will I be able to test and demonstrate it?

6. What resources will I need to build this idea into a viable business?

7. Does my idea solve a billion-person problem or the problem of just a few?

8. Can I envision myself executing on this concept for the next 5 to 10 years?

CHAPTER 2:

FINDING A KILLER BUSINESS IDEA

You know you want to start your own business and be your own boss; great news. However, you don't yet have the perfect business idea - panic not. Here is a method that you can use.

THE METHOD HAS THREE BASIC STEPS:

1. Idea generation

2. Confirm and learn

3. Start small, grow fast

1. Idea Generation: This is about coming up with lots of ideas, writing them down and finding a common thread around which you can start to build an idea. Just remember your business idea doesn't need to be unique, only the way you deliver it.

Doing things you enjoy - that way you will put in the long hours and effort required to build your dream business and minimize the agony. Starting your own business really

CHAPTER 2: FINDING A KILLER BUSINESS IDEA

gives you the opportunity to do something you are passionate about.

So here some questions to ask yourself and scribble the answers down:

- What are you good at?
- What do you enjoy doing?
- What is your experience?
- What's your passion in life?
- What have you always wanted to do?
- What are you hopeless at/really disliked doing?

Once you've done that you need to start looking for common threads and how existing skills and knowledge can compliment your potential business.

You may find that you are good at organizing, love travel and are passionate about wine. Maybe in the back of your mind, you've always wanted to be a travel agent.

Your job so far has been in administration, but you really hate numbers and finance. So looking at this list a possible business idea might be around organizing wine tasting tours for high-net-worth individuals. To address the issue with numbers and finance you might have to think about getting someone else involved either as a business partner or advisor.

IDEAS FOR BUSINESS

2. Confirm and learn: Here we take the raw business idea and start to research its potential. As you start to learn more about the market of the business idea you can start to shape and develop the idea further as well as confirming if it is something that will appeal to you as a long term business.

Look to see if there is a good market for this type of business - Google Trends (It lets you see which is the trend about a topic in a country, region and city! (excellent data to connect to any campaigns facebook ads) and Google Traffic Estimator is excellent free tools for this research.

I personally use the Keyword Planner of Ubersuggest.io as well (https://ubersuggest.io/)

With this tool, I want to go to see which is the critical mass that on the internet is looking for a particular topic.

Ubersuggest is an online tool that, by using the data of Google Suggest, show us all the numbers related to a keyword, which has been typed on Google in a month.

For optimal use of the instrument for the keywords . go to this address: https://keywordseverywhere.com/ubersuggest.html

Download the extension for Google Chrome or Firefox, in doing so, each time on Google you will type a word, it will indicate the exact monthly volume and the cost per click associated with a potential campaign with Google Adwords.

N.B. After installing the extension, go to the web site: https://ubersuggest.io/

CHAPTER 2: FINDING A KILLER BUSINESS IDEA

And there will be the precise volumes of the keywords that you choose, showing all the possible combinations with other search terms.

Type key words in a different way, simply because people do not seek on google all in the same way.

In general for profit:

The more the niche is potentially profitable and the more people will look for it on Internet

In general considers at least 4,000-5,000 average searches per month

On the other hand even if a niche shows many research, do not think that it automatically profitable.

Examine the competition and see how you could be better, different or cheaper. Also look to see how they differentiate themselves.

I use as well Buzzsumo which allow me to run profitable campaign on Facebook. BuzzSumo is basically a **tool of research and monitoring**. Wishing to combine its main features we can identify the following 4 macro-objectives:

- Locate the **contents** more shared on social networks
- Indicate the main *influencer* in relation to particular topics
- Analyze the **competing sites** and return data about its contents
- Notify information and updates on **keywords**, names of **brand, Link, authors** or **domains**

IDEAS FOR BUSINESS

Indicates in the appropriate search bar a topic, and the engine of BuzzSumo will return a list of results that you can order on the basis of the number of shares on Facebook.

Content related to them have been produced, which are the most shared, where and by whom.

So basically, it shows you what are the trend topic of the moment and helps you find new ideas. Through the search for a specific keyword or topic, you have an overview of the most popular content contained on the main channels of social last 24 hours and/or 12 months.

About what we said so far, do some training or maybe get a basic qualification. This will expose you to the environment of the new market and you can quickly see if you enjoy it before investing further.

Talk the idea over with some people you trust. However, most people will be negative about taking the risk. Gets some experience doing some part-time or volunteer work in that sector; Go to a highly informative and fun seminar/workshop to kick the idea around.

3. Start small, grow fast: This is about not being bankrupt within a year! You have found an appealing and desirable business idea. You now understand the market better and have gained knowledge and possibly some experience. So how do you put that into action? I firmly believe you need to test the market for real in a small and part-time way. If this proves successful you can start to build the business and invest more time, effort and money as the business progresses. If your first attempt is not as successful as you wished:

CHAPTER 2: FINDING A KILLER BUSINESS IDEA

    a. You have learned some useful lessons

    b. Adjust the formula and try again.

Developing a business idea that is suited to you could be the best investment of time you will ever make. It is unlikely that your original idea will be the one that you are operating in two or three years time, but the original idea that gets you started will be worth more than your weight in gold.

CHAPTER 3:

HOW TO CREATE A PROFITABLE ONLINE BUSINESS IDEA?

Creating a profitable online business Idea! This is the very first thing any internet entrepreneur should focus on to successfully make money online.

This is the make it or break it factor to be successful online or offline. You may spend a lot of time, effort and money chasing the wrong idea. This step is the most important step.

Frankly, there is no right or wrong way to brainstorm ideas, there are only best practices, common sense and of course some luck. In this chapter, we will present the best practices on how to develop profitable business ideas based on my own experience. Now fast forward to the good stuff.

1. CREATE A PROFITABLE ONLINE BUSINESS IDEA BY INVENTING SOMETHING NEW

   This is rare and the hardest of them all. Like Thomas Edison, who developed many devices that greatly influenced our lives. From the motion picture camera to the long-lasting electric light bulb. If you can picture a

CHAPTER 3: HOW TO CREATE A PROFITABLE ONLINE BUSINESS IDEA?

certain product or service that would make people lives' easier, then you are in business.

2. CREATE A PROFITABLE ONLINE BUSINESS IDEA BY FULFILLING A PERSONAL NEED

If you need a product or a service, be certain that there are other people who are searching for a solution for that exact same problem.

You must always find your way on the market and not just what you like. Listen to the market and discover what it wants.

Start always from real problems or from strong desires that have people out there.

When more a problem does not make you sleep at night, the more it will be easy to make money thanks to a good product, service or information product which is going to fix the problem itself!

Besides "desperate" people do not take rational decisions when they are in this state of mind. So it is easy to sell things, precisely because they tend to take decisions on the spur of the moment.

This is why the niches of this type - where there are serious problems to be solved - are very often the most profitable to work!

Always works in a manner ethics and deliver to people something of real value and that it really improves their life, I recommend.

3. CREATE A PROFITABLE ONLINE BUSINESS IDEA BY MAKING PEOPLES' LIVES EASIER

We are in love with the easy way. We go to Google to find a quick answer and we ask a friend for a recommendation.

We want the easiest and the shortest route to our goals. If you can develop an idea to make people lives easier! They will love you for that.

- Google made our lives easier and now we can find exactly what we need in a blink of an eye. And they are going that extra mile every single day from local search, blog search, Scholar search, image search, movie search, news search and every other kind of search you can think of.

For example:

- Weight loss
- Earning more money
- How to improve a business
- Seduction
- Solve a problem of health
- Resolve a slight psychological problem

4. CREATE A PROFITABLE ONLINE BUSINESS IDEA BY UPGRADING A CURRENT IDEA AND MAKE IT BETTER

Not everyone has the vision to spot a growing trend or a specific need. So it's easier to develop and upgrade a

CHAPTER 3: HOW TO CREATE A PROFITABLE ONLINE BUSINESS IDEA?

current business idea and make it better than the original one.

- Google did this. When they witnessed that search engines were merely displaying search with no clear standards. They developed a search engine that displays results based on user preferences and history by exploiting cookies.

Try to search for any term and make you a friend search for the exact same term with a different computer and you would find different results as Google scans your history and browsing behavior by a very complex Algorithm and displays the most relevant results for you. They grew and became the number one search engine and the number one website on the internet today.

5. CREATE A PROFITABLE ONLINE BUSINESS IDEA BY OFFERING UNBELIEVABLE SERVICE

Sometimes we can't figure out a new business idea or an upgrade to a current business model. Well, the best thing to do is to choose a business model you like. Study it and differentiate yourself not by lowering prices.

- Zappos did it. They started by offering great shoes for sales on their website like the hundreds of thousands of other websites. But they took the customer service to limits never seen before. They would occasionally send you flowers or a present or a voucher for your birthday. They may send your products by speed delivery at no additional costs to you and you would be happily surprised.

IDEAS FOR BUSINESS

Their customer service would speak with you on the phone as long as you need explaining every detail over and over. Actually, there is a documented phone call that lasted for 8 hours! This is how far they took it. The Result? Now they are making over a billion dollar in sales each year! They are the biggest shoe retailer! And their huge customer base does all the promotion and advertising work for them because they were happy and impressed.

6. CREATE A PROFITABLE ONLINE BUSINESS IDEA BY ENTERING A VERY SPECIFIC NICHE

A niche is a group of people sharing a specific interest, hobby or career. You can take a large business idea and break it down to its niche components, study each one and build a business around one niche.

- LinkedIn Is the largest professional social network in the world. They took the Facebook concept and simplified things. They didn't need millions of teens, housewives and TV stars. They chose professionals and entrepreneurs and they built a website specifically designed to serve them.

You can do this. Analysis the big businesses and break them down. Find what would be an interest for you and build a website around it. As an example, I may consider analyzing LinkedIn itself and see the small components inside. Well, you may start a "young professional social network" or an "Executive level social network" or "project managers social network" Decide first. Brainstorm how can you provide an awesome, fulfilling experience for your audience and then build a website to do this and more.

CHAPTER 3: HOW TO CREATE A PROFITABLE ONLINE BUSINESS IDEA?

A niche is a collection of people united by the common desire to solve a specific problem or improve their situation in a specific area.

A commercial niche, plus is a collection of people who are not lumped together only by the requirement cited above, but also:

- They are willing to pay for access to quality information that meets their specific needs

- Have an economic position that allows him to be able to pay your product, service or information product

- Are accessible online

- It is a niche numerically large (at least 4,000 research monthly averages)

7. CREATE A PROFITABLE ONLINE BUSINESS IDEA BASED ON YOUR PASSIONS AND FEARS

Same concept here. If you are passionate about something. There is a good chance that others are in love with it too. If you are totally scared about something you may research and learn to figure a solution and build a website offering that solution.

Or simply a website that offers some sort of support group for whoever suffering from that fear. Trust me it works.

Write down your passions, what you love to read, listen to, or watch. Your dreams, maybe? Or maybe your fears! Write them down. Then rewrite them again. Pin them and look at them every day. Add or delete. I assure you would find

IDEAS FOR BUSINESS

something interesting. 8. Create a profitable online business idea by being weird!

This is not a typo. Although this is not my thing, but some people are flooding their bank account with this

- Million Dollar Homepage If you have ever asked me if setting a website and inviting people to give you money just for putting their logo on a homepage! I would say this will never work! Where is the added value? Well I am wrong this home page collected payments to put brands on the home page "to own a piece of the internet"

OTHER WAYS TO CREATE A PROFITABLE ONLINE BUSINESS IDEA

If your creativity lets you down. Here are some other ways to earn an income by starting an online business.

- Website flipping: Similar to real estate. You build a website. Add content. Attract visitors and offer it for sale on a website like Flippa.

- Web hosting reseller: With a fixed monthly fee you can start selling web hosting service. This can be a profitable business model If you can attract a lot of traffic.

- Review website: Review anything that you are interested in. And offer some Affiliate links. You earn commissions on sales made by your links.

- Content writing: If you are a good writer, set up a website and offer your services. You may join Fiverr,

CHAPTER 3: HOW TO CREATE A PROFITABLE ONLINE BUSINESS IDEA?

> Elance or Upwork people are in a constant need for good writers

This is the only book you would need to find about your big idea! There is not the right or wrong way. As you saw some unrealistic businesses made money. You will never know unless you try. Please stop reading about how to generate profitable ideas for your internet business and start doing what I have told you above.

Let's be practical; Grape a pen and a paper -No laptop pleases- and go through each method described above from inventing something to upgrading a current business idea to embrace your passions and fears or targeting a very specific niche.

Go through each one, brainstorm each one. Write it down. Pin it. Visualize it and you would find your answer. Sooner or later and this is my promise to you.

Some people would argue that they need to test the idea profitability before they start. Well, some people agree and some disagree. I disagree personally. Simply because if you as a person needed something or facing a problem or a certain fear. Be certain that others feel that same way too.

If you are inventing something never done before this testing would do you little good. Ordinary people can't visualize your idea, so their replies would never give you an accurate answer.

An example is when they invented the phone. People never imagined this would be possible and thought their lives are perfect. They invested the mobile phones and now people can't imagine how they lived without them and now their lives are perfect, now they can talk in the street! They invented the smartphones and now you are connected to your social network, your business and to everything.

The idea here is that people can't imagine things. You educate them to accept the new technology. As long as it makes their lives easier, they would be more than happy to listen. You are the creator, create and educate.

CHAPTER 4:

ASSESSING BUSINESS IDEAS THAT YOU HAVE GENERATED

Feasible business ideas are evaluated by analyzing the demand for the product or service, weighing the available resources and looking at the skills, talents, and knowledge you have.

The process of assessing your ideas involves reflecting on all the business ideas and income generating activities you have generated and zero down to three most promising ideas, looking critically at the advantages and disadvantages and basing on your experience and judgment.

To successfully assess the three business ideas that you have selected, you should use a table to tally your results for each business idea and categorize them into columns of skill and competencies, available equipment, access to raw materials, financial resources and sufficient demand. Then use the following questions to guide you:

1. Which of these business ideas matches my strengths?

2. Which idea(s) can help me to achieve my personal goals?

CHAPTER 4: ASSESSING BUSINESS IDEAS THAT YOU HAVE GENERATED

3. Which resources do I need in order to realize the business idea?

4. Which gap am I feeling? Is it a need or a problem?

5. Are there people out there who will buy my product or pay for my service?

You could even ask directly to your potential customers!

Before you try to sell the product you may build a list of potential customers in target (e.g. through a blog), interested in the product, service or information product that you want to sell.

Once you have a list of people interested in a given topic you can directly ask these people what they can affect.

Do questions via email is more immediate and is perceived much better from the people.

Maximum two-four questions well focused otherwise you could piss them off!

Then a mail informal and which it takes up to 20 seconds.

Example of email:

Subject: May you help me? (It is important)

> Hello,
>
> I am creating new material on xy and I need your opinion on some very important aspects:
>
> - What would you like that I spoke in the new material?

- What is your greatest fear about [...]? (alternative: Which is your greatest difficulties in relation to [...]?)

- What have you tried until now which you are disappointed about?

You have my assurance that everything you say will remain strictly confidential.

I thank you in advance for your help!

See you soon.

Your name

Because the survey has value you must have at least a hundred responses. Obviously the higher the number the more it becomes a significant result that get.

To analyze the responses discards the 80% of the responses and keep only 20% of responses for longer.

Who gives an answer more lengthy and thorough feel more clearly and more profound the problem you want to solve with your product.

1. Quantitative analysis

In a sheet of paper or on a Google Form, marked all the problems reported by participants in the survey. For each problem marks how many times it is repeated. At the end put them in order of importance, from the most common to less common.

CHAPTER 4: ASSESSING BUSINESS IDEAS THAT YOU HAVE GENERATED

2. Qualitative analysis

Now read everything from the start and analyzes how people describe their problems. There are phrases particularly incisive? Adjectives or recurring terms?

Collect all these expressions because you will need it when you will write your copy.

1. HOW TO ASSESS YOUR BUSINESS IDEAS BASING ON YOUR SKILLS, TALENTS, KNOWLEDGE AND COMPETENCIES

First of all, you have to assess the extent to which you possess the required skills (manual, personal, social, technical). If you do not have the required skills, you should think about other options like finding someone else with the skills to help you.

If you have to find someone else with the skills, then you should ask yourself further whether you will be able to afford to pay for this person contributing to your business. Remember that additional costs of employing someone might mean a reduction in your profit.

If you find out that the required skill can be performed by you without any problem, that idea should receive a high ranking. But if you discover that your skill level is low or nonexistent as far as the skill required is concerned, then the idea should be rated low.

Secondly, you have to look at the future of the business idea by asking yourself which other secondary skills you have to acquire to fulfill your business goals. And how are you going to get them?

2. HOW TO ASSESS YOUR BUSINESS IDEAS IN RELATION TO THE AVAILABLE RESOURCES

By resources, I mean mainly financial resources, human resources and other inputs like raw materials. You have to think about the start-up and working capital. The good thing online businesses do not require huge sums of money to start. You can start humbly and grow your business.

However, you should take note of the financial resources you need to invest in buying equipment (computer) and start-up expenses. You need to think about having cash that you will use to meet the day-to-day requirements of running your business.

A positive rating only applies when you are able to have all the money required to start the business. And a very low rating implies that you cannot have anything to start the business.

Secondly, you have to focus on other related inputs like equipment and raw materials (e.g. Software). When using certain equipment, you need to possess certain skills. Additionally, you need to look at the availability of the equipment, now and in future, and the challenges you may encounter when using it.

Raw materials are what you use to produce the product. A good business should have a steady inflow of raw materials and their availability is so important. If they are readily available, then give a high rating. But if there are problems or seasonal fluctuations in availability and price, then the rating is low.

CHAPTER 4: ASSESSING BUSINESS IDEAS THAT YOU HAVE GENERATED

3. ASSESSING YOUR BUSINESS IDEAS BASING ON THE DEMAND FOR THE PRODUCT OR SERVICE.

Here you should focus on your unique selling proposition, something special about the idea that can make it more attractive. The demand for a product or service means the extent to which customers want it. You have to take the level of competition in the marketplace.

The demand for a product or service is also related to the ability of the targeted customers to buy. They may have the need for the product or service but when they have no money to pay for it and this means the actual demand is low.

Having gone through the whole process, you will then select one business idea that has received the highest number of scores and note down the points using the points below:

1. What's the idea and what it's status?

2. What market does the business idea address? Are there any customer feedback or testimonials?

3. Why do you believe you have the advantage in the marketplace in relation to the market needs?

4. What's the competition in the marketplace?

5. Who is the team that is going to make the business succeed?

6. What's your long-term vision for your business and the projected returns on investment?

7. What's the estimated total funding required to execute the business plan?

8. What amount of financing are you seeking initially?

Finally, a proper write-up of the analysis of your business idea will be very important for you to further develop a business plan and to convey all the essential information in a more clear and concise manner. It enables you to communicate in a likable, passionate and credible way to capture the attention of others, especially the people you want to support you as you start your business.

CHAPTER 5:

STEPS TO GENERATING YOUR NEXT SUCCESSFUL BUSINESS IDEA

You don't have to be a genius to come up with a business idea. It's the exact opposite! It's really simple to come up with business ideas all the time, however, the challenge lies in coming up with a business idea that works for you and suits your personality and needs.

This is where most people get stuck, many people want to start their own and think about it all the time, the big question is, what business should I start? And it is not a small question, often, the kind of business you are in will dictate whether you will be successful or not.

So, if you have some sort of framework or directions to get your mind focused on business ideas that will suit you and work with your own situation, then you've taken a big step toward becoming successful in business.

1. START THINKING! GET YOUR BRAIN TO WORK.

   Whether you're too busy with your daily routines to take the time to think and reflect on what you want or feel that

CHAPTER 5: STEPS TO GENERATING YOUR NEXT SUCCESSFUL BUSINESS IDEA

your brain is too pressured and lacking the ability to run wild with your imagination, worry not. This chapter has tips and advice that will help you get started with the creative process.

The first step towards creating thinking is understating how the mind works and how to stimulate your brain. I will dig deep into this topic because we might need several books to cover it, but I will briefly mention the key elements.

The brain has two main parts; the right and the left hemispheres, each of these have different functions and work differently.

The right hemisphere is a creative and artistic part, it's the part that appreciates art, it uses shapes, colors, and images to analyze and process information, and it's also the part that controls creativity and the imagination.

The left part is the logical part, it's the part that performs mathematical calculations, looks for causes and effects, uses words to describe and define, and it's also the part that controls speech, grammar, and word order.

For you to be successful in business, you have to have a balance on both sides. You have to be imaginative and creative to come up with business ideas and to come up with creative solutions for business problems.

You also have to be logical to analyze and define business opportunities, calculate business risks and weigh your options to deal with the daily business issues. The brain is

IDEAS FOR BUSINESS

like a muscle if you don't exercise it regularly to get it in shape.

You can't prepare for a marathon by sitting on the couch all day. Common barriers to creative thinking are habits, attitudes, daily routines, lack of confidence or the constant need for guidance from others. A good way to break or overcome those barriers is to be open minded, be receptive to new things, take new challenges, or by simply giving your brain the green light to think creatively. So take the time to think and get your brain stimulated.

Change is one of the best ways to stimulate your brain and discover new ideas. A change of scenery can help you clear your mind off your daily issues and give you some clarity to start thinking creatively, you can go to a garden, beach or anywhere you like and take the time to exercise your brain.

A change of people will also help you, by meeting new people and listening to them talking about their issues or frustrations, you can gain a better insight into their needs and aspirations, which is the basis of any successful business. A change of place will also definitely help you discover new ideas you have not seen or heard of before.

The bottom line is you don't need to go to the other side of the globe to find new ideas, the small changes that you make in your daily will pay in a big way.

2. BUY A NOTEBOOK

Now that you know how to stimulate your brain and get started with the creative thinking process, you need to keep count on your ideas and make sure that you can document them to study and examine them further. In every

CHAPTER 5: STEPS TO GENERATING YOUR NEXT SUCCESSFUL BUSINESS IDEA

business, you can think of starting with a small idea somewhere, from small observations, a frustrating situation, or while taking a shower.

The difference is that those people who had those ideas took the time to think about these ideas and improve on them to create successful businesses. You never know when the inspiration comes, so keep a notebook close to you at all times to write these ideas down whenever they come.

3. FOLLOW YOUR PASSION

Once you start your business, you will spend most of your day for several years doing that business. So make sure you chose a business that you feel passionate and excited about. If you don't like the business you are, chances are, you might not succeed in that business, probably not because you don't have what it takes, but mostly because you might lose interest too easily in the face of the challenges that will come your way.

Starting and building a successful business is no small task, it will be a lot of work, you will face many problems, you will have to deal with situations you never encountered before, so it better be something you love doing. You will find that when things go though, it is your passion that will get you going and make you overcome the hurdles.

If you don't love what you're doing, you will take the first exit when problems arise.

Additionally, if you do something you love personally and understand its motivations, you will be in a better place to understand your customer needs and deliver on them.

IDEAS FOR BUSINESS

Understanding customer needs and their motivations to buy is a key element of understanding your business and ensuring its success.

Having that said, when you decide to take an old hobby into a new business, you have to work out the calculations and make sure that there is enough demand for this product or service, and that people are willing to pay for it. Otherwise, you will end up doing something not many people are interested in.

4. KEEP YOUR EYES OPEN

New business opportunities get born from new situations every day. Keep an eye on what is happening around you, make it a habit of reading the newspaper and identifying new opportunities. You may read that people are complaining from poor health services in your area or the lack of schools in your neighborhood. Talk to your neighbors and the people you know, what is frustrating them? What would they want to change in your neighborhood? Is your neighbor complaining that she needs to drive long distances to get to the nearest dry cleaner? Or is your other neighbor complaining about the lack of groceries in close proximities to where you live? Are your coworkers frustrated that there are no restaurants close to your building work?

If you keep your eyes open to new developments and changes around you, you might capitalize on the emerging opportunities that arise.

You don't need to come up with an original and unique business idea to be successful, often, it's the ideas that have been tested time and time again that prove to be successful,

CHAPTER 5: STEPS TO GENERATING YOUR NEXT SUCCESSFUL BUSINESS IDEA

so look in your area, and see what is missing, it could be your next business.

5. CAPITALIZE ON YOUR STRENGTHS

Most people are good at something. Look at your experiences and career, what is it that you can do well? Did you work in project management for 15 years and know the ins and outs of the business, this is often the best place to start. Most people are afraid to start their own business because they focus on the weaknesses and think that they will fail because of the things they cannot do well. No one is perfect, not every successful business owner is a superman.

Instead of focusing on the things you cannot do well, focus on the things you are good at. What can you do better than others? How are the others doing it? And how can you do it differently? Sometimes, you need a new idea to start a business, maybe a small change to an established idea is your answer.

If your industry is behind other industries in the way it does business, maybe you can come up with a new system to automate their processes or to computerize their records.

Bottom line, look at the things you know best and focus your thinking in these areas. They don't necessarily need to be from your work life.

You might discover that you are good at helping your friends sort their personal finances, so you might think about opening a business where you help individuals plan personal finances.

IDEAS FOR BUSINESS

6. **EXPLORE NEW THINGS**

   As mentioned earlier, change is one of the biggest stimulators of the brain. Even if you don't want to open your own coffee shop, next time you're in one, look at how things are done and think of new ways to improve it.

   Often this thinking might lead you to new ways to improve on your business ideas in your chosen field. Strange enough, your next business idea might be something that never crossed your mind if you haven't been to that business meeting out of town. The more you experience, the wider your options are, leaving you in a better position to generate new ideas and come up with new thinking.

7. **CHECK YOUR BANK ACCOUNT**

   Starting and running your business requires money. Depending on your situation, you need to think of businesses that suit your budget. Everyone's finances are limited, so make sure whatever business idea you come up with is doable.

   If you have a small amount of money, then look into business ideas that do not cash hungry, maybe start small and then grow the business.

   Having that said, there are places where you can get finance for your business, like banks, venture capitals, family, friends and small business associations in your area. Work out in advance the level of finance you are able to raise, and focus on business that will not exceed those limits.

CHAPTER 5: STEPS TO GENERATING YOUR NEXT SUCCESSFUL BUSINESS IDEA

Another key point to consider here, while there are obvious benefits to getting outside financial help to start your own business, those will usually mean that you will have to share your business with others or be in debt. Think carefully about these options and decide in advance if these are risks you want to take or you want to do it completely on your own.

8. KNOW WHAT YOU WANT IN LIFE

Aside from your business goals, think about the reasons you want to start the business in the first place. What is it that you are looking for? What are your goals in life? Are you starting a business to be able to spend more time with your family? To make more money? To be respected among your peers? Whatever your goals are, make sure that your business idea complements these goals and help you achieve them. If your goal is to find more time to spend with your family and do other things, then starting a business that requires you to work 16 hours a day or travel constantly might not be the best idea.

More often than what people think, money is not the real reason why most people start their business. While financial freedom is a big perk of having a successful business, any business can make money, the type of business and how you run your business will be dictated by things other than money alone.

9. CHOOSE A BUSINESS THAT SUITS YOUR PERSONALITY

Are you a morning person or a night creature? Each person has his/her own peak hours of the day. You will find very

IDEAS FOR BUSINESS

few successful bakers or newspaper owners that don't like to wake up in the morning.

If you are not a morning person, avoid businesses that will need you to work in the early hours of the morning.

If you are a night person, then maybe running a night club or a restaurant that stays open till late hours are more suitable for you. Conversely, if you sleep early, running a business that requires you to stay late might not be suitable for you.

Are you an indoor or outdoor person? Do you like working in an office for long hours or can't stand the office and feel that you need on the move all the time?

If you like the office quiet environment, then pick a business that can be done from an office. If you like to be on the move, pick a business that requires you to go to different places and meet new people.

Are you a brain or handy person? People do things differently, some people like to do things that involve thinking and working their brains, other people like to do things that involve craftsmanship and handy work.

Are you a shy or outgoing person? If you are a shy person, then becoming a public speaker might not be the best idea for you. If you are an outgoing person and like to meet new people all the time, having an internet based business might deprive you of that joy.

I think you get the idea, think of your personal traits and attributes and pick a business idea that suits your personality.

CONCLUSION

Read about other people that started their own business: A large part becoming successful involves looking at other successful people and learning how they achieved their success.

Reading autobiographies about prominent and successful business figures and learning how they started their journey will give you great insight on how they did things and what exactly they did to become successful. You find that most of them started from nothing.

Many of them failed at several businesses and had to listen to people that told them they will never be successful. But they stood up and tried again and again until they succeeded. It is not whether you fail that makes you the man you are, it is how you stand up after the fall.

Study their characters, what do successful have in common? How did they achieve their vision? What challenges did they have to overcome? Look for similarities between their stories and your situation right now.

You will find that it is a great source of inspiration and motivation. If others just like you did it, then you can do it too.

Finally, if you found this book useful in anyway, a review on Amazon is always appreciated!

Thank you and good luck with your Business Ideas!

www.ingramcontent.com/pod-product-compliance
Lightning Source LLC
Chambersburg PA
CBHW061228180526
45170CB00003B/1200